Be Kind to Your Banker

How to get the loan or mortgage you need, *and* save hundreds or thousands of dollars in the process.

By Eldon Frost

TABLE OF CONTENTS

Prologue
Introduction

PROLOGUE

Mr. Average considered himself a smart consumer. He had spent weeks reading books about home ownership, bargaining techniques, and choosing a real estate agent. He had since put in a successful bid for a new home.

The sellers had initially wanted $400,000, but after two weeks of negotiation had settled for much less. Mr. Average had only one last step to do – he needed to finalize his mortgage.

Mr. Average decided on a 5-year fixed rate mortgage, so that his payments would not increase for the next five years. After scouring the financial newspapers, he had chosen Bank-X, since they advertised a rate that was 0.5% lower than any other bank. Confident that he had planned well, Mr. Average walked into the bank with a smile on his face and two pieces of I.D. in his wallet. Then he had his interview…

"Have you changed jobs recently?" the lender had asked at one point in the interview.

"Yes," explained Mr. Average. "I didn't get along well with my boss, so I quit. My new boss is better."

"Know anything about Smallville?" the lender later inquired.

"Yes," Mr. Average said. "I vacationed there with my family last year. Great place. Why?"

The day after the interview, the banker had called to congratulate Mr. Average – his application was approved. "Good news," he thought, "and the rate is even 0.3% less than the rate they'd advertised in the newspaper!" Mr. Average thanked the banker, smiling broadly as he hung up the phone.

In reality, Mr. Average wasn't aware of the mistakes he had made; had he known, he could have saved more than $11,000 in the next 5 years alone.

INTRODUCTION

Obtaining loans for the purchase of large items such as cars and homes are amongst the most important financial decisions in a person's life. Yet, despite their importance, there is little information available about how the lending process works.

Most people walk into a lender's office knowing vaguely which qualities will help them get a loan, but are unaware of the all-important details. These details can make the difference between acceptance and decline, and save a borrower hundreds or even thousands of dollars.

This book is a step-by-step guide to the lending process, as viewed from both an applicant's and a banker's perspective. In it, you will find all the information you need to determine not only if you qualify for the loan you want, but also how to find the best place to get it, and most importantly, how to be approved at the best rate.

1

THE CREDIT BUREAU

WHAT IS THE CREDIT BUREAU?

The credit bureau, or simply "the bureau," is actually one of several companies that supply banks, credit card companies, and other financial institutions with information about their customers. In the US, this information is primarily provided by the three nationwide credit agencies: Equifax, TransUnion and Experian. In Canada, Equifax and TransUnion are the largest. Their reports contain information about where you live, where you work, what credit facilities (loans, credit cards, mortgages etc.) you have and how responsibly you use them.

Why is the Credit Bureau Important?

Whenever you sign up for a new credit card, apply for a loan, or even open a new bank account, someone will check your credit bureau file. The bureau's report goes a long way in determining what type of credit access to give you.

Say, for example, that you wish to open up a bank account. If you have a good credit report, the bank will trust you to be a good customer. Therefore, they will arrange your ATM card so that when you make a non-cash deposit such as a check, you can immediately take out some or all of the money you just deposited. If your bureau report is less than perfect, or if you have a history of bad checks, the bank will put a "hold" on your deposits; that is, after you deposit a check, you may not be able to take out your money until several days later.

In personal lending, your bureau report helps decide not only if you are reliable enough to get a loan, but also what kind of rate you will get. Those with good credit history enjoy the flexibility of easily approved credit and low rates, while those with poor credit history may have difficulty being approved or pay premium prices. In short, your bureau report has a big impact on the quality of your financial life.

Why You Need to Check It

Before you apply for a loan or mortgage, or even a credit card, you should first contact the credit bureau and request a copy of your report (more information on how to do this later). Why? First, because bureau reports often contain mistakes. Perhaps your street address is incorrect. Perhaps the name of your employer is misspelled, or even *your* name. Mistakes have a negative impact when you apply for credit.

Even worse, your credit report may contain information that you aren't aware of. For example, it may show that you owe money on a debt that you paid off years ago!

How can the Credit Bureau's Report have Mistakes?

In fact, few people have credit profiles *without* mistakes. Different groups co-actively produce the bureau's reports. If you apply for a bank account, for instance, the bureau supplies credit information to the bank. But, the information you give to your banker is also sent to the credit bureau and used to update your report. In other words, the bureau and bank share information.   Therefore, if a banker spells your name incorrectly ("Smithe" instead of "Smith," for instance) or enters your birth date incorrectly, it may become part of your permanent record.

Things That Look Good on a Bureau Report

What does a bank or lending institution look for when deciding to give you credit? Here is a list of the most important factors:

Former Loans Paid as Agreed. Nothing looks better than for a client to have taken out a loan, made their payments, and paid the loan off as agreed.

Accounts and Loans operating "Satisfactorily." If you have credit cards, bank accounts overdrafts, loans, or any other credit facilities, and you use them within their limits, making your payments on time – this looks wonderful on your credit report.

Using "Revolving Credit" Well Below Limits. "Revolving Credit" refers to credit facilities that you can use over and over again without having to reapply. For example, credit cards, lines of credit, and account overdrafts are all considered "revolving." If you have such facilities but aren't using them to capacity, this looks great on your report. (For example, Bob's credit report shows that his Visa® limit is $5000, but his balance is only $400: this enhances Bob's credit report). The opposite of revolving credit is an installment loan (such as a personal loan or car loan), which can only be paid down but not re-used.

Long Credit History. Jeff, a teenager, has had a student credit card for 4 months. Other than this credit card, he has never used any type of credit before. Due to his short credit history,

Jeff may not qualify for a large loan such as a car loan, even though his credit history is good. The longer his (good) credit history the better, with 6 months being the minimum required.

Things That Look Bad on a Credit Report

Essentially, the things that look poor on a bureau report are the flipside of the things that look good – but the details are important:

Bankruptcy. A former bankruptcy is perhaps the biggest obstacle to receiving the privilege of credit again. After all, a person who declares bankruptcy has a history of receiving money and not paying it back. Having said this, it *is* possible to regain a good credit rating even after a bankruptcy; so, if this describes you, don't despair.

Items Sent to Collections. Collection Agencies are companies that take over the task of getting money from non-paying clients. For instance, say that you owe *Shirley's Catering* $1000 for the food she provided on your wedding day. But, although Shirley has sent three bills and left several phone messages, you still haven't paid. *Shirley's Catering* decides to give your file to a collection agency.

The collection agency will pay Shirley some of the money (ex. $300), and try to contact you to get the rest of the money. If you pay, you will now pay the collection agency instead of *Shirley's Catering*.

You can be sent to collections for just about anything: an unpaid cable bill, traffic ticket, even a lost library book. So, while skipping out on that last utility bill when you move out of an apartment may seem harmless, be aware that it will hurt you later.

Short of bankruptcy, "sent to collections" is one of the worst things that can show up on your credit bureau file.

Payments Made Later than 60 Days. If you are five or ten days late paying your credit card bill, don't let it concern you; you'll have to pay interest charges, but otherwise it won't significantly affect your credit. If, however, you are 60-90 days late on a payment, it will show up on your credit bureau report as a "minor derogatory." A single "minor" will not greatly affect your credit score, but a series of them will. Frequent minors indicate that you are having trouble managing your debts.

A "major" is any payment made 90 days late or greater. A single major will decrease your credit score. Recent late payments (within the previous several months) have the greatest impact.

Suspected Fraud. The possibility of arousing a "suspected fraud" warning is why is it important to ensure that your name, address, workplace and other information in the credit bureau file be correct. If, for instance, your name and SSN don't match, your report may show up in the bureau as "possible fraud." The more information that is incorrect or misleading, the more likely it is that you will be considered a fraudster.

Inquiries. Every time you open up a bank account or apply for credit – even a department store card – it will show up on your bureau report as an "inquiry by a financial institution." Normally, this is not a concern. However, if you have several inquiries on your report in a short period of time, your lender (and the bureau) may wonder what you are doing. Have you been applying for many credit cards, with the intention of racking them up before declaring bankruptcy? Have you had to change financial institutions because you wrote NSF checks or did fraudulent transactions? Are you experiencing a cash-flow crisis, and using new debt to pay your existing bills? To avoid seeming suspect, it's a good idea not to apply for many credit products in a short period of time (1 year or less), especially prior to applying for a major loan or mortgage.

On this note, if you use a mortgage broker or auto lending specialist, tell them to never, *ever* "shotgun" your application. "Shotgunning" occurs when a broker sends your application to several financial institutions at once. Doing so may get you approved for a loan or mortgage, but will also ruin your credit score for several months. If using a mortgage broker or lending specialist, tell them to selectively apply to 2 or 3 financial institutions (maximum).

High Utilization. "High Utilization" refers to a person's tendency to use credit products to their limits. For example, if Bob has a MasterCard® with a $5000 limit, and his balance is $4989, he has a utilization of 99.8%. For lenders, "high utilization" means that you are likely to use credit if is it given to you, and therefore you shouldn't be given too much.

In some cases, it's actually *better* to have more credit cards (or other credit facilities) than you actually need, *as long as you don't use them.* For instance, if Bob (from the example above) only has a MasterCard, his utilization is 99.8%. If, however, Bob also applies for a Visa® and is accepted with a limit of $6000 – *but doesn't use it* – Bob's total utilization is now only 45% ($5000 MasterCard limit + $6000 Visa limit = $11,000 available, but using only $4989). As in the above example, adding new, unused credit can actually improve your eligibility.

As with anything else, however, one can get too much of a good thing. Having *many* credit cards, even if unused, is considered a sign of potential irresponsibility. The best method is therefore to have two or three credit cards, but carry a balance on only one (or none) of them.

THE STORY OF SUSIE SMITH

Susie Smith is a well-organized individual. She always pays her bills on time, always keeps her credit card balances low, and has been working for the same company for 15 years. About two years ago, she got a promotion and was transferred to the city, receiving a large bonus. Recently, Susie decided to buy a new car, and walked into her local bank to get a loan. "This should be easy," Susie thought.

An hour later, Susie was in shock – her loan had been declined! "What could have happened?" Susie wondered. She decided to order a copy of her credit bureau file. When it came in the mail a week later, Susie was again surprised.

She had gone to the dentist just before leaving her hometown two years earlier – something she'd completely forgotten about. Instead of sending the bill (for $152) to her new address in the city, the dentist had mistakenly sent the bill to her old address. Because the bill went unpaid, the dentist eventually sent the bill to a collection agency. Now, Susie has a "major derogatory" rating on her credit bureau report, telling potential lenders that she is unreliable!

Susie Smith's Bureau Report

On the following pages is a copy of Susie Smith's credit report. Notes and comments have been made in ***bold italics*** to indicate important points. Being able to read and understand a credit report such as this one is essential to understanding the loan approval process.

SUSIE A SMITH
123 ANYWHERE ST
ANYTOWN, PL

PERSONAL IDENTIFICATION INFORMATION

The following personal identification information is currently
showing on your credit file.
Your date of birth and social security number have been partially
masked to protect your personal information.

Date File Opened: 06/27/95

Name: Susie A Smith
Current Address: 123 Anywhere St., Anytown PL 12345
Date Reported: 07/01
Previous Address: 1050 OldPlace Ave., Oldtown PL 12345
Date Reported: 05/01

Birth Date/Age: 01/XX/1979
Social Security Number: 987-65-4320

Current Employment: ACME Services Ltd.
Previous Employment: Baier Holdings Ltd.*
Prior Employment: Sales, Friendly Electronics
*Susie's previous employer was actually "Bayern Holdings Ltd."
Susie should contact the bureau to change this name, as it will
not match information that she provides to lenders in the future.

Information provided in this report also includes information
reported under the name(s):
No listing

- 1 -

CREDIT INQUIRIES ON YOUR FILE:

Following is a list of members who have received a copy of your credit file for credit granting or other permissible purposes. Addresses are available by calling 1-877-323-2555.

DATE	REQUESTERS NAME*	TELEPHONE
05/16/07	CITI	(866) 222-3556
12/23/06	HSBC BK	(250) 492-2554
06/23/01	GM VISA	(416) 982-3559

The Citi request occurred on the day that Susie applied for a loan. The HSBC Bank request is from when Susie opened a bank account. The final request was when Susie applied for a Visa credit card.

The following inquiries are for your information only and are not displayed to others. They include requests from authorized parties to update their records regarding your existing account with them.*
In other words, the following items were not due to Susie's application for any credit. They are merely requests for updated information by existing lenders, and so do not count as "credit requests" on Susie's file.

DATE	REQUESTORS NAME	TELEPHONE
04/06/07	US COMM CU	N/A
03/22/06	CITI (NOT DISPLAYED)	(866) 222-4444
03/08/07	HSBC BK (NOT DISPLAYED)	(866) 444-2222

CONSUMER INTERVIEWS AND OTHER SERVICES:
You contacted our office in 05/11 to request a review of your credit file.

CREDIT HISTORY AND/OR BANKING INFORMATION
The following information was reported to us by the organizations listed below. Information is received every 30 days from most credit grantors.

- 2 -

AMERICAN EXPRESS (800) 668-XXXX last reported to us in 05/11 rating your revolving account as R1, meaning paid as agreed and up to date. At that time the reported balance of your account was $0. Your account number is XXX...900. This account is in your name only. The account was opened in 11/00. The credit limit or highest amount of credit advanced was $5600. Your account has been reported to us over a 72-month period. The last payment or transaction made on this account was in 05/06.

CITI VISA (800) 983-XXXX last reported to us in 04/11 rating your revolving account as R0, meaning too new to rate or opened but not used.* At that time the reported balance in your account was 0$. Your account number is XXX...404. The account was opened in 06/01. The credit limit or highest amount of credit advanced was $5000. Additional comments: Inactive Account.

The account is not rated, and so does not add any value (good or bad) to Susie's credit record. If Susie is trying to build a strong credit rating, she should consider making a few purchases on the card, then paying it off. This will result in an active R1 or "good" rating for the card and probably improve her credit score.

US COMM CU (800) 877-XXXX last reported to us in 04/11 rating your revolving account as R1, meaning paid as agreed and up to date. At that time the reported balance of your account was $0. Your account number is XXX...001. This account is in your name only. The account was opened in 02/98. The credit limit or highest amount of credit advanced was $1000. Your account has been 30 days past due 2 times(s). Your account has been reported to us over a 72-month period. Additional comments: Personal line of credit. Your account was previously rated R2, meaning one payment past due in 05/03.*

Although the card was rated R2 in the past, this is nothing to be concerned about. R2 ratings are not considered "major" problems. The account is now rated R1.

- 3 -

Harris Bank (403) XXX-2865 last reported to us in 02/09 rating your instalment account as I1, meaning paid as agreed and up to date. At that time the reported balance on your account was $0. Your account number is XXX…713. The account was opened in 06/04. The credit limit or highest amount of credit advanced was $8732. The minimum payment terms are $151. Your account has been reported to us over a 52-month period. The last payment or transaction made on this account was in 05/08. Additional comments: Student loan. Account paid.*
An account such as this – rated I1 and paid as agreed – looks great on a credit report.

PUBLIC RECORDS AND OTHER INFORMATION:

The following information was reported to your file on the date indicated.

A collection was reported in 10/06 by CBB COLLECTIONS SERV in the amount of $152. Collection Status: Unpaid. Reference: UPTOWN DENTAL 0509. Date of last payment: 03/04. Collection agency reference number: 01022750655.*
This is the item that is killing Susie's credit score. Although Susie's other credit items are all rated R1 or I1, this unpaid collection (for only $152) is severely affecting her rating. After this item is paid, a note will be added saying, "paid." Although the item will still show on the bureau report for six years, her credit score will vastly improve, immediately.

RETENTION PERIOD OF DATA

CREDIT INQUIRIES TO THE FILE An Inquiry made by a Creditor will automatically purge three (3) years from the date of inquiry. The system will keep a minimum of five (5) inquiries.
The remainder of the credit file explains how long each item of information remains on your file (negative things like bankruptcies and collections are usually 6 years) and gives phone numbers for things like suspected fraud or identity theft of your account.

END OF REPORT

Contacting the Credit Bureau

In case you haven't already guessed, the most important step you should take before applying for a loan or mortgage is to *CONTACT THE CREDIT BUREAU.* Contacting the bureau – Equifax, TransUnion or Experian – allows you to check your personal file for mistakes. It may also remind you of a long-lost bill that you were unaware of, but may be ruining your credit rating.

In the USA, to obtain a copy of your credit report, simply go to the website: www.annualcreditreport.com. *You can obtain a free copy of your credit report every year.* In Canada, both Equifax.ca and TransUnion.ca will mail you a copy of your credit report minus you score (description only) for free. If you wish to obtain a copy that includes your credit score, you must pay a fee. For the purposes of this book, the free copy is sufficient.

I've Got My Bureau Report. Now What?

The next step toward your loan depends upon the condition of your credit bureau report. After reviewing your credit information thoroughly, choose the option below that best describes your situation:

- **If your report has any item that has been "sent to collections," but is otherwise good (like Susie Smith), refer to Appendix A for solutions.**
- **If your report has one or more items that have been "sent to collections," as well as any other "majors" (ex. unpaid bills longer than 60 days), see both**

Appendix A and B for the steps you should take. Also read section D.

- If your report has a former bankruptcy, see Appendix C and D for the steps you should take.
- If your report has any errors – such as name spelling, address, birthday etc. – contact the credit bureau directly to correct the information (info on how to do this is part of the letter you receive). If information about any existing loans, credit cards, etc. is incorrect, you must contact the issuer (ex. bank) and get them to send a letter to the bureau to change your information.
- If you bureau report is solid, with no "majors" or errors, you are in great shape and can continue on to the next section: Part 2, Where to Apply – And When

2

WHERE TO APPLY – AND WHEN

WHERE TO APPLY

In the financial industry, "rate shopper" is derogatory slang for a customer who shops around to several financial institutions for a loan, then picks whichever one offers the lowest rate. Of course, choosing a loan should involve price, but there are other factors to consider as well.

First, choose a major financial institution with a good reputation. Lenders that do payday loans or other "sleazy" products are more likely to give you a loan – even with bad credit – but can also cause significant problems. Most "nightmare" financing stories come from low-quality lenders.

Low quality lenders, also known as "risk lenders," typically charge sky-high rates and hidden fees. These fees, when added to the already high interest rates, result in overall rates that are far beyond what most lenders charge. Risk lenders typically don't care if you can afford your payments – only if you can get approved so they can make their commissions. In addition, other institutions see risk lenders as second-class. If you have a major product such as a car loan or mortgage from a low quality lender, most banks will assume that you had to get your loan there because you were declined everywhere else. In other words, using low quality lenders can result in financial prejudice against you, and may hurt your chances of getting loans in the future.

For their lower rates, respectability, and the potential for future business, a major financial institution should always be your first choice.

The second and most important factor in deciding where to have your loan or mortgage is to choose a lender with which you have an existing relationship. "Existing relationship" doesn't mean that you have to know the lender personally or play poker with him on Friday nights (although it helps). An existing relationship refers to any company with whom you have done business.

Say, for example, you have had a bank's credit card for several years, and the card is in good standing. Or, maybe you have had a bank account for years with no bounced checks or other problems. In either of these cases, you have a solid existing relationship with that financial institution, whether you realize it or not.

Some banks have their own internal reliability rating systems that they use in addition to the credit bureau. Although your credit bureau record score may not be great, your credit record with that particular bank may be good and they may consider you to be a reliable customer. Good, long-standing customers are not only more likely to be approved for loans, but also get preferred rates. For large loans and mortgages, the more products you have with the bank, the lower your rate will likely be.

A Word on "Posted Rates"

One of the most frequent mistakes that customers make when shopping for a loan is to walk into a bank with which they have no relationship, just because that bank advertises a good rate (ex. *Old Bank* has a 5-year fixed mortgage rate of 6.0%, but *Friendly New Bank* has a rate of only 5.0%).

The rates that you see advertised on the Internet and in newspapers are known as "posted rates." Posted rates are similar to "manufacturer's suggested retail prices." You may have noticed that the suggested retail price of a certain item may be $100, but when you go shopping, all the stores are selling the item for $80. The suggested retail price is just that – a suggestion. The same goes for posted rates.

Good customers almost never pay posted rates, especially for large loans or mortgages. Therefore, don't rely on advertised rates to make your decision.

WHEN TO APPLY

If you have a steady income, perfect credit, and are applying for a loan that is easily within your budget, then you can apply for a loan anytime you want. For many people, however, timing the loan interview has a lot to do with the success of the application.

It is important to remember that loans are done on a "today" basis. It doesn't matter if you will be receiving a large inheritance next month – until it's in your hands, it doesn't count. It also doesn't matter if you plan to pay off that credit card next payday. The only thing that matters to lenders is what they can see today. Therefore, it's your responsibility to make "today" look as good as possible.

The Case of Stewart Student

Consider the case of Stewart Student. Stewart goes to the University of Michigan, with the school year beginning every September. During the summers, Stewart works for his father's business. At the end of each summer, Stewart usually has several thousand dollars in savings, but by the end of the school year has almost nothing left in his account.

If Stewart applies for a credit card in June, he can show a bank balance of $8000, plus show a (temporary) monthly income of $2000. If Stewart applies for a student credit card in April, he will show a bank balance of $220, plus no income at all. Guess which time of the year is better for Stewart to apply for a credit card? That's right – the end of summer.

Just like Stewart Student, most people have times of the year – or even times of the month (ex. after payday) – that show the best financial picture. Always apply for a loan at a time that presents your best image; doing so can make the difference between acceptance and rejection, and will help you get a lower interest rate.

Credit Card and Line of Credit Balances

A smart "best practice" is to pay off, in full, your smallest credit card and line of credit balances *before* going to see a lender. Having small balances on your credit cards or lines of credit exaggerates your monthly payments, making the amount of money you owe seem larger. The reason for this is the "either/or" clause found in the statements of most credit facilities.

A typical credit card statement says that the minimum monthly payment is "3% of the outstanding balance *or* $10, *whichever is greater.*" Likewise, a typical line of credit (LOC) says that the minimum monthly payment is "2% of the outstanding balance *or $50, whichever is greater.*" If you carry a $100 balance on your credit card, 3% of $100 is only $3 dollars. But, because the minimum is 3% *or* $10, the $10 charge applies instead. To see the effect that this clause has on your minimum monthly payments, see the example in the following chart:

Andy		Betty	
Balance Owing	Minimum Payment	Balance Owing	Minimum Payment
Visa $500	$10	Visa $200	$10
Amex $500	$10	Amex $100	$10
LOC $2500	$50	LOC $200	$50
MC $2000	$40	MC $2000	$40
Total: $5500	**$110**	Total: $2500	**$110**

Even though Andy owes $3000 more than Betty, *their minimum monthly payments are exactly the same.* And, because credit applications are done on a "today" basis, the bank's computer assumes that Betty needs to make payments of $110 per month, every month. Therefore, to avoid overstating your monthly payments, pay off your small credit card and line of credit balances before visiting the lender (bring your payment receipts).

The following table illustrates the dramatic effect this can make:

Betty – 2:00 pm (same as above)		Betty – 2:10 pm, after payment	
Balance Owing	Minimum Payment	Balance Owing	Minimum Payment
Visa $200	$10	Visa $0	$0
Amex $100	$10	Amex $0	$0
LOC $200	$50	LOC $0	$0
MC $2000	$40	MC $2000	$40
Total: **$2500**	**$110**	Total: **$2000**	**$40**

As you can see, Betty has paid off only 20% of her credit balance ($500 of $2500), but her required monthly payments are 64% less! This not only looks good and feels good, but also makes a huge impact on your debt servicing levels (which we will learn about in Section 4 – Estimating your Probability of Success). Debt servicing is how banks decide if you can afford to make the payments on your new loan.

Showing smaller required monthly payments goes a long way toward making you worthy of a loan. So, if you are able to pay off your smaller credit card and line of credit debts before visiting the lender – do it!

3

PREPARING FOR THE LOAN INTERVIEW

If you were going to help your neighbor fix his plumbing, you probably wouldn't grab a screwdriver, walk into his house unannounced and yell, "I'm here!" Instead, you'd probably arrange for a good time to come over, and arrive with a toolbox filled with the tools you will need. Going for a loan interview is no different – it requires preparation. Yet, people continue to show up for loan interviews with nothing more than two pieces of ID and a smile, completely unprepared for any questions the lender may ask.

In order to make the loan process go as smoothly as possible, you must be prepared.

NECESSARY ITEMS

List of Tangible Assets

Tangible assets are the things you own that can be sold easily, for a determinable value. 401(k)s, stocks, bonds, mutual funds, and money in bank accounts are tangible "liquid assets" (the best kind). Their value can be determined almost to the dollar, and they can be sold quickly and easily.

Other tangible assets are things like vehicles, boats and trailers, properties and homes. Although these cannot be sold as easily, they can be taken to a dealership or real estate agent and sold in a short period of time, and they keep most of their value. On the other hand, you may have a great stereo system and a collection of furniture from a local craftsman, but from the bank's perspective, these are not tangible assets. The bank couldn't easily sell them, and their value is not easy to determine.

Good lenders are not pawnshops – only tangible assets count in your loan application.

Intangible Assets	Tangible Assets
Sound system Dining Table Home Computer 10-Yr Old Vehicle Most antiques	Home/Property Business Assets Stocks & Bonds 5-Yr Old Vehicle Painting by Picasso

A Complete List of your Debts and Obligations

Debts and obligations include loans, lines of credit, credit cards, dept store cards, gas station cards, bank account overdrafts, and any other credit facilities. For credit cards and other forms of "plastic," write down both the credit limit and the current balance. For loans, record the amount owing and monthly payment. If you are a co-signer for someone else's loan, write down the details of this loan as well.

It is important that the list be complete, including even credit cards with a 0 balance, or that you rarely use. Modern lenders use computers that check your credit bureau file. If your debt list is incomplete, the credit bureau will display a warning that says "undeclared debt." A single missing item is not a disaster. But if several debts are missing from your list, the banker has good reason to be suspicious: either you are intentionally misleading your banker, or you are financially disorganized.

In the real world, it's not uncommon for customers to have thousands of dollars of debt that they don't mention during the loan interview, mistakenly thinking that the banker "will never know." While this gives lenders something to gossip about at the water cooler, it certainly doesn't help an application. Declaring all your debts makes an application *more* likely to be approved.

A sample debt calculation for "John Doe," as well as a blank form for your own use can be found in *Appendix E: Liabilities Worksheet (Sample and Blank Form).*

Proof of Income

Bring two current and consecutive pay stubs, direct deposit slips, or a year-end taxation form to prove your income. If you are just beginning a job and do not have these items, ask your employer for a letter of employment, written on company letterhead, with details of your wage/salary, regular hours, owner or supervisor's signature and contact phone number.

If you are a commissioned salesperson, self-employed (including private doctor, accountant etc), or sole proprietor/partner, 2-3 years of your most recent financial statements are usually required. If you don't have 2-3 years worth of information, the lender may not be able to use your income in the application at all! Most lenders require financial statements that have been confirmed by a notary or accountant, or have been submitted for tax purposes, as well as a recent taxation notice to show that your taxes are up-to-date.

Identification

The list of acceptable identification varies, but a person must have two pieces of I.D., at least one of them "primary." Any I.D. issued by the federal or state government is acceptable as primary I.D., and anything issued by a bank, insurance company or national institution is acceptable as secondary. At most institutions, identification does not have to include a photo, but must include both name and signature.

Address History for Work and Home

Most people don't bring their work address to the loan interview, and they either have to come back with it, or make their lender find it. Avoid this complication by having it ready. Most lenders require 3 years of address history for both home and work, *including zip codes*. Lending computers use zip codes to do things like determine your neighborhood and verify your work status.

Social Security Number

The credit bureau uses your SSN to correctly identify you. If you give the wrong SSN or omit it altogether, the bureau may pull up a report on the wrong person with the same name – or be unable to find any information for you at all.

Other

If you have recently married, bring an original or notarized copy of your marriage certificate to provide proof of your new status and/or name change.

If you are applying for a mortgage or a loan related to your home (such as a Homeowner's Equity Line Of Credit), bring a recent appraisal of the property, or your most recent property tax assessment. These documents estimate the value of the property, and also provide the necessary legal description.

TOO MUCH WORK?

To some people, all this preparation may seem like a lot of work. Well, you have to ask yourself, "Would *I* lend a large amount of money to a stranger without any information?"

Having complete information for the loan interview has several benefits: it saves you time (in the long run); it gives the impression that you are organized and professional; it greatly increases your odds of approval; and, it can save you hundreds or even thousands of dollars from reduced interest rates. Most people find that taking the time to come prepared is definitely worth it.

PRE-INTERVIEW CHECKLIST - SUMMARY

O Credit Bureau Report checked and updated

O Lowest-balance credit cards paid off (if possible)

O Complete list of tangible assets

O Complete list of debts and obligations (A blank worksheet is available in Appendix E: Liabilities Worksheet)

O Proof of Income

O Two pieces of I.D.

O SSN

O 3 years of Address History for Home

O 3 years of Address History for Work

O Copy of Investment Statements (if applicable)

O Other (name changes, property information, or other information if applicable)

4

ESTIMATING YOUR PROBABILITY OF SUCCESS

THE "BIG 5"

When you apply for a loan, lenders don't look at income, credit rating, debt level etc. independently – instead, they put the pieces together to get the "big picture." Someone can have a great salary, for example, but a lousy credit score – indicating that although they may make a lot of money, they still don't like to pay back what they owe. In order to make accurate judgments, major lenders review 5 separate qualities.

1) Good Credit – do you always pay your credit cards and bills on time? Do you have a history of successful loan repayment? Are you using your credit facilities well within your means?

2) Good Income – Is your income reasonable compared to others your age? Being 21 and working part-time in a hamburger restaurant is perfectly fine. If you are 40 and work part-time in a hamburger restaurant, it may indicate a problem – especially if you are the family's main income earner.

3) Financial Maturity – Are you planning for the future? If so, you should – at a minimum – have the equivalent of two month's salary available for emergencies.

4) Personal Maturity – Do you quit your job and move every 6 months, or have you been working for the same company and living in the same house for several years? Travel and adventure are part of youthful enthusiasm, but by middle age you should at least be reasonably stable. If you move or change your job, it should be for a good reason – like higher pay or a promotion.

5) Net Worth – Net worth is the dollar value of all your assets, minus the dollar value of all your debts (net worth = assets – debt). Over time, you should build assets faster than debt, resulting in a progressively increasing net worth. If you have a good income and long work history but low net worth, it may indicate that you are living beyond your means, or are simply irresponsible.

Bonus – Collateral – collateral is an item such as a car, home, property, or investment that lenders can take as security against a loan. If you do not make your loan payments as agreed, the lender can take the collateral.

In order to get a loan, you don't need *all* of these qualities, but you do need to have at least three of them. Banks require the three qualities to be from the BIG 5. High-risk lenders (such as payday loan companies) don't care about character as much as banks, so will allow you to get a loan with only one from the BIG 5, as long as you offer collateral.

High-risk lenders approve loans more easily, but compensate by charging higher prices and taking collateral. If a 5-year fixed-rate mortgage is 6% at banks, a high-risk lender will typically charge between 8-14% for the same thing. Although a 2% interest rate difference may not sound huge, for a $200,000 mortgage (over 25 years) this difference equals about $76,500!

Take a realistic look at yourself: do you have three of the qualities from the "BIG 5" list? If you do, a bank will probably be interested in your business. If not, you may have to wait until your conditions improve, or use a high-risk lender and pay much higher prices (I highly recommend the former).

CAN YOU AFFORD IT?

DEBT SERVICING - THE "DSR RATE"

You may have three qualities from the Big 5, but how do you know if the amount you are asking for is realistic? After all, even someone with sparkling credit history is unlikely to qualify for a $5 million personal loan if his or her income is only $30,000 per year. The answer is to use the same formula that the banks use – the DSR rate. Calculating it takes only a few minutes, and will tell you if your loan request is reasonable (and safe).

DSR, or "Debt Service Ratio," compares your required payments to your regular monthly income. Ideally, your required monthly payments should be no higher than 35-40% of your gross monthly income (income before taxes).

In the previous sentence, note the word *required*. If you have a gym membership and high-speed Internet access, these are regular monthly expenses, but ones that could be cancelled at any time. Only payments you are *required* to make are used in DSR calculation.

As an example, let's use Andy and Betty. Andy and Betty both want to buy a new car and are applying for a loan. Using a "payment calculator" on their bank's website, they estimate that their monthly payments will be about $400 per month. Can they afford it? They can do a rough DSR calculation to find out, as shown in the following chart:

Andy			Betty		
Product	**Balance**	**Required Monthly Payment**	**Product**	**Balance**	**Required Monthly Payment**
Visa	$500	$10	Visa	$200	$10
LOC	$2500	$50	LOC	$200	$50
MC	$2000	$40	MC	$2000	$40
Rent		$550	Mortgage	$200,000	$1200
			Property Tax		$100
Gym		$0 (can cancel)	Gym		$0 (can cancel)
New Car	$20,000	$400	*New Car*	$20,000	$400
Total Required Monthly Payments: **$1050 month**			Total Required Monthly Payments: **$1800 month**		
Andy's Monthly Income (before tax) **$3200**			Betty's Monthly Income (before tax) **$3200**		
DSR **$1050/$3200 = 0.328 or 32.8%**			**DSR** **$1800/$3200 = 0.563 or 56.3%**		

In the example in the previous chart, Andy is at less than the maximum 40% DSR (and is at the optimum "less than 35%" level), so he can afford to pay for the new car loan, and will likely be approved for it. On the other hand, Betty is far over the 40% DSR maximum, and will likely be declined for the loan. This is probably a good thing, since paying the loan would be a struggle for Betty.

What Income can be used for the DSR Calculation?

Every bank/lender has different policies for what can and cannot be included as income, but here are the standard guidelines:

- Salary, hourly wages and pensions can always be included as income.
- Commissions and bonuses may only be included if you have received them for 2 years or more, or if they form the main part of your salary (ex. "commission only").
- Overtime pay can only be included if the amount has been stable or increasing for 2 years or more.
- Investment income can only be used if the amount received is stable and predictable.
- Alimony payments may only be included if they have been received regularly and are likely to continue (a lender may ask for court documents).
- Income from a second job (if your primary job is full-time) can only be included if the second job has been stable for 2 years or more.
- Rental income is usually marked down to reflect the risk that a rental unit may become unoccupied for some time – for example, if you receive regular rental income of $1000 from a basement suite in your home, the lender may only use 75% of that amount in the calculation of your income.
- If your rental income is from a second property (not your residence), then lenders use a different DSR calculation, so don't worry too much if you do a rough DSR calculation and the result seems high! Your lender will do a revised DSR calculation.

A Warning about Approvals

Most people assume that if a bank approves them for a particular credit limit or loan amount, it must be safe to use that amount. On the contrary, *if you have a good credit history you will be able to obtain credit for amounts larger than you can actually afford.*

The DSR calculation is a generic formula that doesn't take into consideration personal circumstances. If, for example, you are a single professional with a large income, having a DSR of more than 40% may be quite comfortable. On the other hand, if you have a moderate income and are married with two children, having a DSR of 40% may require you to clip food coupons to avoid bankruptcy.

Keep in mind that 40% is the *maximum* amount a person should borrow, and that for most people, maintaining a DSR of 40% or higher means flirting with disaster. *If you want to stay safe, think about the monthly payment that would be comfortable for you, and go into the lender's office with this payment amount in mind.* Don't take out a loan that is larger than you need, just because you can!

5

THE INTERVIEW – TECHNIQUES AND TIPS

STEP 1 – MAKE AN APPOINTMENT

As a rule, always make an appointment to see a lender. First of all, lenders are busy, and if you walk in unannounced they may not (will probably not) be able to give you the time required to do things right. Secondly, some banks have special computer codes for "walk-in clients," reflecting increased risk for these clients: walk-ins are, statistically, more likely to commit fraud than those who have made an appointment! Therefore, your first visit or phone call to the bank should be nothing more than to set up an appointment.

When you make your appointment, be sure it's at a time when you will not be rushed. Booking off 20 minutes from your lunch break may seem like a good idea, but is usually insufficient. Lenders must find out what you need & what you want to use the funds for. They have to ask questions about your work, credit, legal issues, lifestyle etc., and then finally make a recommendation. All this is hard to do in less than 30 minutes: an hour may be necessary.

Rushing through a loan interview is not only annoying for your banker, but may cause them to miss information vital to the deal's approval. So, be patient, and leave plenty of time for questions.

STEP 2 – ACE YOUR LENDING INTERVIEW

4TK – The Winning Technique

4TK stands for "*T*ell *t*hem what *t*hey need *t*o *k*now." For lenders, having trust in a client goes a long way. To promote this sense of reliability, the best thing a client can do is to mention anything negative, or supply any explanations, *before* the lender asks. This is called, "full, true and plain disclosure," and is what every lender wants.

Nicknames. If you use a nickname or anything other than your legal name, still use your legal name for the application. If you've been using your nickname so long it has become your identity, apply using your nickname but also give your real name, to ensure that your lender knows that both refer to the same person.

    Example: William Thomas Smith never liked the nickname "Bill." So, to avoid being called Bill, he always introduced himself using his middle name, "Tom." Tom's passport and driver's license show his name as "William," but his banking cards and credit cards show his name as Tom. Tom should apply using his legal name ("William T. Smith"), but let his lender know that he usually goes by the name "Tom."

Recent Job or Address Change. In some circumstances, frequent job or address change is not unusual. For example, dam supervisors and construction workers may move each time a project is completed. Young people commonly change jobs and addresses until they settle into a career or buy a home. For most others, however, frequent job change is negative.

Job change could indicate that you are running away from creditors or landlords, that you are avoiding the law, or that you frequently get fired. Therefore, from the credit bureau's perspective, recent moves and job changes are something to be investigated.

If you have moved within the last 6 months, you should be ready to offer an explanation. A good client should have a legitimate reason, such as "to be closer to my family," "to take advantage of a good job opportunity," or simply "to move to a better area." Ensure that *your* reason reflects good judgment.

Spending on Intangible Assets. If you spend a lot of money on intangible assets that hold their value (such as coin collections, antiques, or designer furniture), give this information to your banker to show "where your money goes." The lender will probably not be able to use the information in your calculation of net worth, since such things are usually of no value to a bank. Nonetheless, you can at least show your banker that your money is being spent on items that hold their value, and not on frivolous spending or nights out at the casino.

As you can see in the chart below, Bill has more tangible assets (assets that the bank can count) than Fred, but adding the antiques into Fred's list creates a better impression than if he had simply not mentioned them.

Bill Williams – age 35	Fred Williams – age 35
Car $15,000	Car $15,000
Mutual Funds $15,000	Mutual Funds $5000
Savings Account $1000	Savings Account $1000
Checking Account $500	Checking Account $500
Antiques $0	Antiques $50,000

Negative Credit Bureau events. Even people who keep meticulous track of their finances can have negative events in their credit bureau history. For instance, perhaps you misplaced a library book so the city sent you to collections for payment. Or, maybe you forgot to pay an outstanding water bill when you moved. If you have an event such as this in your credit history, explain the circumstances to your lender. Specifically, explain a) why it happened b) what you've done to fix it, and c) why it will not happen again. Most importantly, do this during the initial interview, *before* they view your credit information.

A lender who believes your story can make negative credit bureau items less important to the approval process. In many cases, what may have been an "automatic decline" by computer can be changed into an approval.

Inquiries on your Bureau. Nothing makes a banker more nervous than viewing your credit file and seeing that you have had credit inquiries by several financial institutions in the last month! Fraudsters are known to obtain as much credit as possible, rack up their debts to buy luxury goods, and then declare bankruptcy or move.

If you have several "hits" on your bureau report in the last few months, indicating that you have applied for new financial products, it decreases your credit score significantly. For this reason, it's a good idea not to apply for new credit cards or other forms of non-essential credit within several months of when you apply for a big loan or mortgage.

If you already have many inquiries on your credit bureau because you've been shopping for a good deal, be sure to explain that to your lender.

Other Interview Tips

Don't Talk Product. During your interview, tell the lender what you want to do with the money, but don't specify what type of loan you want. For example, don't walk into the lender's office and say, "I want a line of credit" or "I want a car loan." Instead, just say what you need (ex. "I need money to buy a car.") The reason is that the most obvious choice (ex. a car loan to buy a car) is sometimes not the best choice.

Rather than specify the type of loan you want, let the lender give you options. An experienced lender at a good institution will choose the best option for you and "structure" it so that you get the best rate.

Create a Sense of Competition. Tell the lender that you are also speaking with another financial institution, even if you aren't. A lender is more likely to offer you the best rate if there is any chance of losing your business to a competitor. Simply mentioning that you are "also checking out the bank down the street" can shave hundreds of dollars off your loan payments.

Dress Code. The days when you had to go to the lender's office wearing a suit and tie are definitely over. These days, the lending process is mostly done by computers and based "on the numbers." However, modern lending still involves the human element.

If a computer turns down a loan application, the banker has two choices: either accept the decline, or fight to have your loan accepted. If you came into bank wearing old gym pants, were marginally rude, and had a mediocre credit history, it's unlikely that the lender would bother to go further with your application. However, if you were well dressed, polite, on time – and still had a mediocre credit history – your lender is far more likely to make a personal recommendation for your approval.

Dressing nicely and being likeable may just convince your lender to go the extra mile for you.

Contact Numbers. Always leave a cell phone number or alternative contact number. Often, after reviewing your loan application, a lender will have several additional questions that didn't come up in the initial interview. Leaving a work number or cell phone number where you can easily be contacted can therefore speed up the lending process significantly.

Lying and Fraud

Never lie during a loan interview. This may seem obvious, but it is astonishing how many people do it – especially when faced with a question they think will hurt their chances of approval.

In reality, stretching the truth is likely to *decrease* your chances of approval. Lies often don't make sense when viewed as a whole. Maybe, for example, you say that you moved to town last year, but your credit report shows you've been working at the same location for two years. Maybe your income doesn't seem right for your position. Maybe you say you only have one line of credit but the bureau report shows that you have three. People who lie under pressure usually make mistakes that make their stories seem ridiculous.

Worse than "under pressure" fibbers are those who perpetrate intentional fraud. Fraudsters have been known to alter employment documents and income tax forms to show higher income, claim ownership of property that isn't theirs, and borrow money from friends or family to show large account balances. There is no limit to fraudster's ingenuity. Such ingenuity, however, typically ends in disaster.

Firstly, fraud is a criminal offence that could result in jail time. More practically, if you receive a loan that you can't actually afford, you are only hurting yourself. You may just cheat yourself all the way into bankruptcy.

The Story of Juanita – Juanita came into the bank to get a car loan. When the banker asked her if she owned her own home, she said, "yes," even though the mortgage and title were actually in her father's name. She thought that by claiming to own the home (the asset), she could show a larger net worth. However, because Juanita claimed ownership, the banker also added the mortgage payments to her application, making her fully responsible for the debt. Due to this extra debt, Juanita's car loan was declined.

A SAMPLE LENDING INTERVIEW

Acing a lending interview doesn't require rocket science, just a little bit of diplomacy, keeping in mind the techniques and tips offered earlier. Think of a lending interview as a casual job interview. If you wouldn't make a particular comment during a casual job interview, you probably shouldn't say it during a loan interview either. Sound positive, and give good reasons for your actions.

Lending Interview: Mr. Footmouth

Lender: "So Mr. Footmouth, I see here that you changed your workplace five months ago. Was there a reason you changed your job?"

Mr. Footmouth: "I didn't like my old job. My boss was a real jerk. So, I decided to quit and look for something else. My new company is much better. I really enjoy it."

Lender: "By the way, do you know anything about a line of credit at X-bank?"

Mr. Footmouth: "A line of credit? I thought I told you about that already?"

Lender: "Hmmm. I must have forgotten that you mentioned it. By the way, for your new loan, what amount are you looking for?"

Mr. Footmouth: "As much as I can get, I guess."

Lending Interview: Mr. Goodline

Lender: "So Mr. Goodline, I see here that you changed your workplace five months ago. Was there a reason you changed your job?"

Mr. Goodline: "My job was alright, but I heard that Acme Company has a much better work environment with the same pay. So, I decided to apply and I got the job. I really enjoy it."

Lender: "Great. By the way, do you know anything about a line of credit at X-bank?"

Mr. Goodline: "A line of credit? I'm sorry I probably forget to mention that one. I rarely use it."

Lender: "OK, that's no problem. For your new loan, what amount are you looking for?"

Mr. Goodline: "I was hoping for $X, with payments of about $200-250 per month. I think I could go higher, but an amount with a payment in that range would be the best."

In the above examples, Mr. Goodline clearly has the advantage. Mr. Footmouth showed financial immaturity by quitting his job *before* applying for a new one, just because he didn't get on well with his boss. If he does this again, it is a risk to his income and therefore a risk to the bank. Mr. Goodline, in contrast, quit his job for the same reason, but worded his answer to reflect that he "moved up" into a better job category.

When asked about the undeclared Line of Credit, Mr. Footmouth choked and gave a reply of, "I thought I told you about that?" (In reality, the most common reply to this question). Mr. Goodline, however, explained that he forgot because he "rarely uses it," which is a good reason.

And, where Mr. Footmouth is clearly desperate to get the loan and doesn't care what his payments are, Mr. Goodline has given some thought to his loan, and knows how much he is comfortable spending.

When you go for *your* loan, be like Mr. Goodline: take your time, relax, and give honest but diplomatic answers.

Telephone and Internet Banking

In the last several years, telephone and Internet banking have come of age. You can now apply for loans and mortgages without ever leaving your home, often obtaining excellent rates. But there are several downsides to this convenience as well.

Because the telephone and Internet process is relatively impersonal, your application will be based primarily on your credit score. If you have great credit, this is good news; if you don't, your application will probably be declined.

You should also be selective about whom you obtain credit from. Online lenders offer low rates to entice new clients, but lenders that exist only in cyberspace may be difficult to contact and difficult to pay. For example, if you want to receive payment from an online bank, you may have to either transfer the funds to a "real" bank, or get a cheque sent to you in the mail. In addition, some online banks are "risk lenders" that may be more willing to lend you money because their contracts make it easier for them to repossess your assets.

Finally, those who use Internet banking should be cautious about fraud. Never apply for a loan by replying to an email offering great rates. Mass marketed emails are often from organized groups whose sole purpose is to obtain your personal information.

6

I'VE BEEN DECLINED – NOW WHAT?

People naturally feel rejected when they are declined for a loan, not realizing that in many cases, being declined is a *good* thing.

Reputable lenders have a responsibility not to lend money to someone if it puts them in a dangerous financial position. Maybe *you* think that repaying the loan will be easy. But, when your lender takes a hard, unbiased look at your finances, he decides otherwise. By declining your loan, your lender may be doing you a favor.

In addition, remember that "no" is only for today. A woman with excellent credit history may be declined for a loan if she is currently unemployed, or is working for a company that is downsizing. If the same woman walked into a bank two weeks later with a new job, she may be approved for the same loan as a preferred customer. Fortunes change.

Learning from the Experience

A question you should always *ask your lender* is, "Why was I declined?" Many lenders will avoid a direct answer to this uncomfortable question at first, but press them a little to find out – after all, this is your information! It could be something simple, such as bank policy that is not a reflection of any major problem. For example, maybe qualification for a mutual fund loan requires a minimum income of $50,000, and your income is $42,000.

Financial counseling is part of a lender's job. A good lender will always, when asked, state alternatives to help you get the loan you want, or make suggestions on how to reach that stage in the future.

Finally, this book is itself a guide to loan approval. If you have read this book thoroughly, you should already have a good understanding of the reasons for your decline. Take the time to re-read relevant sections and make a strategy for your future.

Co-Signers / Guarantors

Lenders will often suggest that although you don't qualify for the loan yourself, you can proceed with a co-signer or guarantor. Many people think that a co-signer or guarantor is someone who just "helps" you get the loan: this is incorrect.

A co-signer is someone who, along with you, is legally responsible for the debt. A guarantor is someone who guarantees that they will pay if you are in default. Although legally different, lenders usually use the two terms interchangeably.

A co-signer must be someone with good income, a stable job, and good credit history – all the qualities of a good borrower. If your co-signer has bad credit history, there is no point in asking that person to be your co-signer!

Co-signing a loan is a big responsibility, so if you ask someone to be your co-signer or guarantor, don't do it lightly. And, *never* ask someone to be your co-signer unless you are 100% committed to making all your payments on time.

7

I'VE BEEN APPROVED

FINAL RATE BARGAINING – ON LARGE LOANS AND MORTGAGES

Many people have bank accounts or other business at more than one financial institution; if this is you, there is something important you can do before loan closing in order to get the best rate. After your loan is approved, but *before coming in to sign the paperwork*, ask your lender this question: "If I move my business (ex. investments, bank accounts, GICs etc) to your bank, can I get a better rate?"

Many lenders will be happy to grant you a better interest rate in return for more of your business. Please note, however, that I stressed asking for the lower rate *before* the paperwork is done and ready to sign. Printing and preparing lending documents takes time. Depending how much work the documents are to change, the lender may just say "no" to your rate reduction request simply to avoid redoing everything.

Below is a conversation of someone doing it correctly:

Banker: "Hi Carl, this is *Mr. Banker*. I have good news. I am just calling to let you know that your loan has been approved, and that you just need to come in to sign."

Client: "That's great. I can come in anytime Friday afternoon."

Banker: "2:00pm OK?"

Client: "2 o'clock is good. Now, what interest rate are you giving me?"

Banker: "You've been approved at x%. That's 1% lower than the regular rate."

Client: "Alright. Now, currently I have some investments and a bank account at *Other Bank*. If I move my investments and account to your bank, what kind of rate discount could you offer me?"

Banker: "Uh, please wait a minute and I'll check (client holds as banker asks senior lender, manager, or uses pricing software). I can offer you an additional .75% discount. That's the best price we can offer for this amount."

Client: "That sounds fine. Please do the paperwork and I'll see you on Friday."

If the lender doesn't offer a better rate, or doesn't seem interested in your extra business, ask to be introduced to the branch manager (nicely), and explain your situation. Generally, managers care more about the bottom line than regular employees, and may fight harder to get your business. They are also usually able to discount prices more than regular employees.

The bargaining should be very cordial and polite. If you are loud or abusive and "demand" that your rate be reduced, the bank may not even want you as a long-term banking customer (Banking code says that if a customer is abusive, that customer does not need to be served again.)

You will not always get a discount by bringing over new business, since you may have received an excellent rate from the start. If your banker refuses to reduce your rate, and you *reasonably* think it should be lower, you have the option to try your luck at another institution.

"High Risk Pricing"

If a lender charges you *more* than the regular rate, the reason may be that you have received "risk pricing." Risk pricing is given to clients who are able to support the loan, but who present greater risk to the bank than the average customer (perhaps you are new to your job, have a low income, high debt level, weak credit history, etc.). If your bank offers you a loan with an interest rate higher than advertised, you've probably received risk pricing. If in doubt, simply ask you lender.

CLOSING DAY

Closing day is the day when you will go to the bank to sign any legal documents related to the loan. Sometimes this is the same day as the loan application, but usually not. On closing day, you will also have to make several decisions related to the operation of your loan, including payment schedule, payment method, and whether or not to take insurance. While these may seem trivial compared to the loan itself, they are important, and so are reviewed next...

Creditor Insurance

Some people hear the word "insurance" and immediately decline the offer, thinking that it is similar to an extended warranty. But, creditor insurance can be valuable. Banks offer insurance on their credit products for three primary reasons: 1) it's profitable for them 2) it reduces a clients chances of defaulting on the loan; and 3) it helps the bank keep a good image by protecting clients from personal disaster.

Life insurance pays out the remaining balance of the loan or mortgage if a client dies, thereby eliminating any debt for loved ones. Many people decline life insurance because they have 401(k)s or investments that are enough to pay off the loan, should anything happen. However, do you really want your family to use all their savings to pay out an outstanding loan? Life insurance can pay off the outstanding debt in the event of death, while also allowing your remaining family members to keep their assets.

Disability insurance makes the minimum monthly payments on behalf of a client. If you become ill or disabled, the plan will take over your payments until you recover, usually for a period of up to two years (check the individual plan for details). Some companies offer similar plans to their employees, but such plans are often inadequate, covering only a minimum amount. For example, work-based disability insurance covers only injuries derived from work (not outside the workplace), and may pay an employee only 60% of their current income in the case of a claim.

If you already have adequate insurance, then you don't need it on your loan. However, if you don't have adequate coverage, creditor insurance is a convenient way to protect you and your family. *And, because the banks make money on insurance, you may be able to obtain an additional discount off the interest rate of a mortgage or large loan, partially offsetting the cost.* Ask about possible discounts if you are interested in obtaining insurance.

Payment Schedule

Loans can be paid weekly, bi-weekly (every 2 weeks), semi-monthly (for example, on the 1st and 15th), or monthly. Some money managers recommend paying the loan on a more frequent basis (ex. weekly), in order to save on interest charges.

However, the most important consideration is to match your loan payment schedule to your income payment schedule. For example, if you get paid on the 1st and 15th of every month, also make your loan payable on the 1st and 15th of every month. Matching your loan payments to your income stream makes paying a loan surprisingly painless, and lets you avoid making payments on days that are financially inconvenient (such as the day before payday).

The Amortization "Safety Net" Principal

When you have your loan interview, your banker will probably ask you, "Over how many years do you want to pay this off?" or "How many years will your mortgage be?" The premise of the Safety Net principle is simple: given a choice, *always choose the longest amortization (time to pay off the loan) that is available without a fee, as long as making extra payments is an option.*

Say, for example, that Susie is approved for a car loan of $20,000. Her banker tells her that she can choose to pay it off over any time period from 1 year to 5 years (12-60 months). And, she can make extra payments at any time without penalty fees.

If Susie chooses a shorter amortization period (ex. 1-3 years), her monthly payments will be higher, but she will also pay off the loan faster and pay less interest. If she chooses the longer amortization she will have lower monthly payments, but take longer to pay off the loan and pay more in interest charges.

Susie wants to avoid paying large amounts of interest, and she feels that she would be able to pay off the loan in three years, so she is strongly considering the three-year amortization option. Yet, this option will make her required monthly payments higher. What should she do? The Safety Net Principal makes the decision easy.

The Safety Net Principal says that she should take the longest amortization (5 years) that has the lowest monthly payments. This gives her the highest degree of safety, since the payments are easily affordable. However, since she is also allowed to make extra payments without penalty, she should also make extra monthly payments for an amount that would equal the 3-yr option *if she had chosen it.* These extra payments can be made in the branch, using online banking, or at some banks can be set up to be completed automatically. In an emergency, this extra payment (unlike the loan payment itself) can be cancelled.

The result of the Safety Net is shown in the following chart:

$20,000 Car Loan	
Susie – 3 yr amortization	**Susie – 5 yr "Safety Net" amortization**
Required Monthly Payment $627	Required Monthly Payment $406
	Auto Extra Monthly Payment $221
Total Monthly Payment $627	**Total Monthly Payment $627**
Total Interest Cost (3 yrs) $2562	
Paid off in 3 Years	

As you can see from the previous table, the required monthly payments are lower for the 5-year amortization. If Susie has any financial difficulties in the next 3 years, she can simply cancel her extra payments and make the required payments only: if she does this, she will still maintain her good credit rating. If she does not experience any financial difficulties, she will pay off the loan in 3 years as planned.

Safety Net amortization gives you the best of both worlds – it allows you to pay off a loan early and save money on interest charges, while also providing maximum flexibility by keeping required payments low.

Payment Method

For revolving credit – such as credit cards or lines of credit – it's wise to set up automatic payments. By signing a simple form, you can arrange for either the minimum payment or the full balance to automatically be paid from your bank account every month. Setting up automatic payments takes the worry out of remembering, and is especially convenient if you go on vacation or become ill. In addition, auto payments force you to honor your debt, keeping your credit rating intact.

8

LOAN AND MORTGAGE MAINTENANCE

If you have received your loan, congratulations! However, you will find that getting a loan is rather like having a baby; although it may have seemed difficult, the greatest challenge (and reward) is still to come. Here are some tips and suggestions to keep both you and your banker happy.

Payments "On the Principal"

Save your pennies. Making extra payments, over and above your planned payments, takes a huge cut out of the interest you pay over the course of a loan. Regular payments are part principal (the amount you borrowed) and part interest. Extra payments, however, go entirely toward the principal. Over the long term, principle payments can save you hundreds or even thousands of dollars.

These days, even closed mortgages allow some extra payments without penalty (usually 10-15%), and even a few hundred dollars a year makes a big impact. Lines of credit and most car loans can be paid in part or in full at any time without penalty.

Be sure to read the details of your loan, or ask your banker to explain the extra payment options available to you.

To ensure that your extra payments are processed correctly, be sure to state that you are making a payment "on the principal."

$250,000 over 25 years at 6% Total Interest Paid
With no extra payments
$188,443
With one $600 extra payment per year
$175,371
With a $50 extra payment every month
$174,767

Cash Crunch

People with financial troubles tend to "hide," not explaining their situation to their banker or spouse or anyone else: this is the worst thing you can do. If you expect to have difficulties making your regular payments, *contact your banker* as soon as possible.

To make your finances affordable, lenders may allow you to do things like skip payments, make interest-only payments, or extend the amortization (time to pay the loan). Best of all, your credit record won't suffer a bit.

Remember, bankers don't want you to stop paying them! Your banker *wants to make it easy for you* to have healthy finances. If you ever have financial troubles, your banker should be your first call.

Example – Dave Williams. Dave was in dire straights. His wife was having a baby and would have to take maternity leave soon. Not only would their family income be lower, but there would also be many new expenses. Dave didn't know if his pocketbook could handle it, and he was worried. What if he couldn't keep up his mortgage payments?

Dave called his banker, and the banker informed him that because he was having a "major family event," he could skip his mortgage payments for up to 3 months without penalty. Dave was relieved – three months without mortgage payments would allow him to save enough money to avoid a cash crisis.

If Dave had not spoken to his banker and merely skipped the same payments on his own, his account would have been "in arrears," hurting his relationship with his bank and his credit score.

Buyer's Remorse

A friend of mine, we'll call him "Jim," worked as a bike courier and had a good (though not a great) income. He brought me over to his apartment one day to show me his brand new convertible car.

"Isn't it great!" he said. "It was really expensive, but it's so nice. Actually I was looking for something a little cheaper, but the sales guy showed me this one and I fell in love with it. It's beautiful!"

He went on, explaining how great the car is and what wonderful features it has.

"The payments are about $900 per month," he said. "It's quite a bit – almost as much as my rent. But it's a great car."

The more Jim talked, the more I realized he was trying to convince himself that the car was affordable, even though he knew it wasn't. Finally, I said to him, "You're right, it's really a great car. But, I think it's a bit expensive. If you got a cheaper one and saved the extra money, you'd be able to go out and do a lot more."

Jim looked like a huge weight had been lifted from his shoulders – I had said exactly what he was hoping someone would say.

"Maybe you're right," he said, "it's a great car, but I should get something cheaper."

The next day, he took it back to the dealer and traded it in for a car that wasn't as beautiful, but was within his budget. Even though he lost a few hundred dollars in the exchange, he was happy to have rid himself of his overwhelming debt.

It's nice to get a great car or home, but making the payments should always be both affordable *and comfortable*. If your payments are causing you to lose sleep, consider downgrading or selling that asset before it kills you!

9

IN CLOSING

Making large purchases, such as a car or a home, are amongst the most important financial decisions of your life. Ensure that when you make any financial decision, you are prepared to the fullest extent possible. That means learning what is required (such as reading this book), and taking no shortcuts in the process. Saving thousands of dollars is easy if you take the time to do things right!

APPENDIX A

TEMPORARILY BAD CREDIT

Many people who normally take good care of their finances have what I call "temporarily bad" credit. That is, their credit is generally excellent, but they have at least one "glitch" that is hurting their credit score. For example, someone who always pays his bills on time, but didn't pay (or wasn't aware of) a long overdue library book, and who was subsequently reported to the credit bureau. Fortunately, temporarily bad credit is easy to fix. The solution depends on whether the glitch is your fault or the issuer's fault.

Erroneous Charge

If the charge against you is an error, or illegitimate, call both the credit bureau and the collection agency (if applicable) and let them know that you are disputing the charge. The bureau will put a note on your file, stating that the item is "in dispute." Any lender who views your file will now see that the reason you haven't paid is because of a disagreement. If you eventually win the dispute, the negative item will be removed and will not become part of your credit history.

Be aware that disputing an item on your credit file may take a long time to be resolved. If the dispute is for a small amount of money, consider paying it to improve your credit score, even if you disagree with the charge.

Correct Charge

If the charge against you is legitimate, contact the debtor and arrange for repayment. If the overdue debt has already been sent to collections, call the collection agency directly to arrange for repayment (ex. if an overdue dentist's bill was sent to collections, you now pay the collection agency, not the dentist).

After the debt has been paid, tell the collection agency to contact the credit bureau to update your file as soon as possible. Wait 2-3 business days, then call the bureau to double-check that your credit history was indeed updated. You do not need to ask for a full copy of your credit report, but simply ask the bureau if your file has been updated by the collection agency in the past few days.

At this point, the credit agency may frighten you by telling you that although the item is now paid, it will remain as a "black mark" on your record for several years: this is true. However, despite the historical "sent to collections" that remains on your file, your credit rating will nonetheless improve substantially and immediately.

A person who has one historical black mark on their file but who is otherwise reliable will still enjoy an excellent credit rating.

Once the glitch on your credit report has been paid, removed, or is now officially "in dispute," you are ready to go back to Section 2 of this book, entitled "Where to Apply."

APPENDIX B

CURRENT DELINQUINCIES WITHOUT BANKRUTPCY

Step 1 – Sustainable Lifestyle Change

If you have several delinquencies on your credit report, there are two common causes: either you are living beyond your means, spending money that you don't have and are therefore unable to make your payment obligations; or, you may simply be irresponsible, combined with a lack of planning. Usually it's a combination of these two. Does this frankness sound harsh? It should. Thousands of people waste their hard work and money living a lifestyle that only brings them deeper and deeper into debt. Don't be one of them. Change your employment and earn more, or change your lifestyle and spend less.

Financial change is rather like going on a diet. If your diet plan is to eat nothing but grapefruit three times per day, it is destined to fail. You will have initial success, but after a few days or a few weeks, you will become tired of eating nothing but grapefruit and go back to your old eating habits, gaining all the weight back and possible more (since you may binge after having deprived yourself of what you like). Financial change works the same way.

If you try to save money by never going out with friends, never going out for a coffee, never taking a vacation, and never buying anything for yourself, you have done the equivalent of a financial grapefruit diet. Such a situation can only last so long before it becomes unbearable and you return to your previous habits. To be successful, financial change must be sustainable.

Step 2 – Lower your Credit Card Interest Rates

Due to high interest rates, paying off credit card debt can take years. So, the first step of our debt management plan is to reduce your interest rates. To do this, simply call the toll-free line of any credit card or department store card that you have, and *ask* them to lower your interest rate! These days, competition in the credit card industry is fierce, and many companies offer low rates to entice you to use their card over a competitor's. Therefore, credit card companies will often offer a low rate for a set amount of time, usually 6 months. For example, a company may offer 6 months at 4% interest (instead of the usual 18.5% interest) if you move debt from a competing card to theirs.

Of course, not every card company will lower your rate. But if you have been a good customer, some will make you a competitive offer – and that is enough to make your call well worth the effort. In other cases, you may have to pay a small annual fee (ex. $25) to reduce the interest rate on your credit card; if you carry a balance of more than a few hundred dollars, it is a good value.

Step 3 – Restructure your Banking Debt

The third step in debt management is to change your payment options so that your required payments are as comfortable as possible. To do this, visit the office or call the toll-free service line of any major lender that you have business with (loans, mortgages, lines of credit etc). Tell them about your current cash crunch, and ask for assistance to help keep your payments affordable.

In many cases, a lender can lower your interest rate, extend your loan, or give you a new loan with a better rate. In banking, such changes are known as "restructuring the debt."

If you are unsuccessful negotiating this yourself, you may wish to contact a certified accountant who will call companies to restructure debt on your behalf. Of course, accountants charge a fee for this service, but if you have substantial debt their fees will be worth it.

Despite popular belief, bankers don't want to sell your house or repossess your car. Banks don't want to lose your business, or develop a bad reputation by collecting customer's assets. If they believe you are reliable, most lenders will work with you to help you manage your debt.

Step 4 – Arrange Automatic Monthly Payments

The best way to build a great credit history is to never be late making your payments. And, the easiest way to make all your payments on time is to make your payments automatic: virtually all credit card companies and financial institutions have forms for this. You simply sign the form, write your funding bank account information, and choose either "pay full balance every month" or "make minimum payment every month." The debt will thereafter be paid automatically. To get auto payment forms, ask for one from your bank, or call your credit card company and they will send you an auto payment application form with your next statement.

Step 5 – Transfer your Balances

If you have several credit cards or lines of credit, it is to your advantage to transfer the largest balances to the cards with the lowest interest rates (See Step 1 for beginning this process). Low interest rates mean that more of your payment will go toward the principle (the money you owe) and less to the interest charges that accumulate during the month.

You can transfer funds between cards by using "credit card checks," which are sometimes sent in your monthly statement, by taking out a cash advance from the low interest card and paying against the higher interest card, or by calling the credit card company directly (they will supply you with the paperwork to make the transfer).

In the example below, Carol has successfully transferred her balance from her high-interest Visa card to her lower-interest MasterCard.

Carol - Before	Carol - After
Visa at 18%, $5000 owing, $5500 limit	Visa at 18%, $3000 owing, $5500 limit
MasterCard at 10.8%, $4000 owing, $6000 limit	MasterCard at 10.8%, $6000 owing, $6000 limit
Amex at 12%, $1000 owing, $1000 limit	Amex at 12%, $1000 owing, $1000 limit

Carol has moved an extra $2000 from Visa to MasterCard, which will save her $144 a year in interest.

Step 6 – Pay off your Debts

The debt to pay off first (ex. loan or credit card) is the one with the lowest amount owing – not necessarily the one with the highest interest rate. Paying down the smallest debt first has a positive psychological effect, as you will see your debt shrinking noticeably month by month.

After a credit facility has been fully paid down, cancel it if you have not used it properly in the past (ex. had payments more than 90 days late). Ignore letters from the credit card companies when they try to sign you up for replacement cards, even if they offer lower interest rates.

Paying off a credit card – and then canceling it – looks great to a lender and also improves your credit score. In addition, canceling credit facilities that have been misused makes them *seem* to be further in the past and not part of your current character.

Sample - Carol's Plan

Carol (see the chart in Step 5) has 3 credit cards with balances owing. She has arranged automatic minimum monthly payments for all 3 cards, and is now making extra monthly payments – of whatever she can afford – on the card with the lowest balance (AMEX). She has also adjusted her lifestyle, and isn't using her credit cards for any new purchases. Just a few months ago, Carol dreaded her monthly credit card bills. Now, she is finding satisfaction in receiving her statements and seeing her balances decline. After her AMEX card is fully paid, she will start paying extra on the card with the next-highest balance (VISA). She will keep paying down her debts, one by one, until they are either fully repaid or until her debt level is comfortable.

Warning: Debt Consolidation Loans

Debt consolidation loans are loans where debt from various lenders is combined into a single payment with a lower interest rate. For example, someone with debt on several credit cards may pay these off by obtaining a single large loan. By combining balances into one low–interest debt, the required monthly payments are substantially lower and the debt is paid off faster.

Although the idea behind debt consolidation loans is good (combining debts into one payment at a lower rate), debt consolidation loans for revolving credit, such as credit cards, are typically unsuccessful.

Recall that revolving credit is credit that can be used over and over again. A credit card is "revolving" because as soon as the debt is paid it is available to be used again. A car loan (regular installment loan) is non-revolving because once the loan is paid it cannot be used again without reapplying.

Debt consolidation loans typically use non-revolving credit (a loan) to pay off revolving credit (credit cards). However, experience shows that once their credit cards have been paid off using the loan money, customers usually end up reacquiring their credit cards and racking up their debts again, resulting in both credit card debt *and* loan debt. In order to avoid this trap, *only consolidate revolving credit debt using other existing revolving credit.* For example, use your existing low-interest credit card to pay off your other credit cards. You are thereby not obtaining any new debt products, but merely rearranging your existing debt into more manageable payments. Steps 1-6 of this chapter explain the process in detail.

Rather than using another debt to pay off your debts, instead you must implement a *major lifestyle change* (see Step 1 or this section).

STORY: THE TURNAROUND OF CHARLIE PARTY

Charlie Party had a great time in university, but had a string of bad luck after graduation. He became two months behind on his student loan payments, and was unable to make his credit card payments for more than three months. Charlie finally got a new job, but when he applied for a car loan, he got declined. Charlie had no car, no girlfriend (his girlfriend broke up with him because he couldn't afford to take her out), and no life. He decided to make some changes.

First, Charlie moved into an apartment with a lower rent, even though he would now have to commute an extra 20 minutes by bus to get to work. Then he contacted the credit departments of all his debtors to restructure his debt, cut down his morning espresso and muffin from five days a week to two, and cut down the number of beer nights with his buddies from three to one. He used the savings to help pay off his debts. Charlie Party made sacrifices.

Charlie got all his payments up to date (the student loan company let him pay interest-only until his situation improved), paid off two of his lowest balance credit cards and then cancelled them, and started making his regular payments on the others (as a result they are now rated "satisfactory"). He also saved $1400 for a down payment on a used vehicle. Charlie put his financial situation in his control.

Six months after his initial interview, Charlie went back into the bank, was upfront and honest about his prior payment troubles, and explained the sacrifices he had made to improve his financial situation. Charlie got the loan.

If you have completed Steps 1-6 of this section, with Step 6 being completed six months ago or longer, you are ready to go to Chapter 2 – "Where to Apply, and When."

APPENDIX C

BANKRUPTCIES

Make no mistake about it – bankruptcies are a big hurdle to overcome. You may feel that *your* bankruptcy is different – that it happened for reasons beyond your control, and that you have no intention of it ever experiencing it again – but the facts tell another story.

Statistically, people who claim bankruptcy once often go on to claim bankruptcy a second time. Bankruptcies typically indicate a "weak financial character:" that is, someone who likes to get loans and live a nice lifestyle, but who is reluctant to pay back the money if things go wrong. This may or may not describe you, but the bank has no way of knowing this – they just look at the facts. And the facts say that borrowers with historical bankruptcies are risky.

Moving away from bankruptcy and proving that you are good for a loan or mortgage doesn't happen by accident: it takes effort and a plan. Your credit record must be methodically re-established, piece-by-piece.

The most important first step in any bankruptcy is to do a post-mortem analysis. Sit down and give some hard thought as to the causes of your bankruptcy. And, be aware that no single reason is ever the answer. You may first believe, for instance, that the reason you became bankrupt is because you lost your job. Yet, many people lose their jobs and don't become bankrupt. More likely, it was because you lost your job, had high levels of debt, and had no savings or backup plan. Think off all the reasons that caused you to declare bankruptcy, and write them down.

Next, mitigate each and every reason for the bankruptcy. If your bankruptcy began because of an extended illness or disability, do you now have disability insurance? If the first step in your bankruptcy was a divorce, are you now free of the fees and payments of the divorce? If the bankruptcy occurred due to job loss, are you now in a more stable industry? If not, do you have job loss insurance? Do you have two months of income in savings or cashable investment in case of an emergency? If the bankruptcy was initiated by high credit card debt and living beyond your means, have you established a budget and are you sticking to it? Mitigating bankruptcy means eliminating the causes – and therefore the likelihood – that it will happen again.

If the causes of your bankruptcy have been mitigated, and your bankruptcy was discharged 1 year ago or longer, you are ready to move to Appendix D – "Re-establishing Credit."

APPENDIX D

RE-ESTABLISHING CREDIT –
BE A SMART MONEY
MANAGER

Step 1 – Financial Maturity

Re-establishing credit involves doing all the things that smart money managers do, the first and most important steps of which are emergency planning & asset building.

Smart money managers have money either in a savings account or in cashable investments in case of emergency – a good guideline being at least 2 month's worth of living expenses. With emergency cash in savings, things like being laid off from work or having your car engine die become nuisances rather than financial disasters.

Asset building involves building up your level of "tangible assets." From a banker's perspective, a tangible asset is anything of value that could easily be sold by a bank. So, while a large-screen home entertainment system has value, it is not an asset as far as a bank is concerned. Increasing your tangible assets – such as mutual funds, 401(k) s, stocks and bonds, homes or condos, and cash – are all signs of good financial planning and responsibility. Even a small investment shows that you are thinking about the future by buying things that increase in value.

Personally, I have seen people with bad credit history – but good jobs – walk into a bank, apply for a $10,000 loan with

$1 in their bank account, and wonder why their loan was turned down. Smart money managers don't live "on the edge" of financial ruin. They plan for emergencies by having about 2 month's worth of living expenses in savings or cashable investments, and spend their money on assets that hold or increase in value over time.

Step 2 – Credit Products

Overuse of credit, such as carrying high balances on credit cards, is a major contributor to bankruptcy. So, in order to prove your creditworthiness you must show that you are not "addicted" to credit. That is, that you are not using credit to support your lifestyle, and are able to handle carrying a credit card without using it to its limit.

If you kept your existing credit (ex. credit card) through your period of bankruptcy or credit trouble, then you already have some credit established. If you currently have no credit facilities, you must try to get one and show that you can use it properly. There are a couple of credit facilities that are the easiest to obtain.

The first easily obtainable credit item is a 401(k) loan. A 401(k) loan is a small, short-term loan that allows you to buy 401(k) investments. Once the 401(k) investment is made, it will allow you to either get a larger income tax return, or at least owe less tax. For the banks and lenders, it's a low-risk item because the money is leant, then goes straight into an investment in the same institution. In order to qualify, you will need to show that you have enough income to support the required monthly payments. You also need to show that you have some savings, to prove that you are currently not living above your means. If you have zero dollars in your bank account at the end of every month, how will you be able to pay off a new loan?

The second easily obtainable credit item is a low limit credit card from a "risk lender." A risk lender is one that specializes in giving products to customers that are high risk. How do you recognize which lenders specialize in high-risk? They are not major banks, they are usually open late and on weekends, and their advertising expresses their "convenience."

Risk lenders charge higher rates for their loans and credit cards, but at least you may be able to get one, even with a poor credit history. If you qualify for such a card, make a few small purchases with it, pay it off in full, and then don't use it again for a few months. This ensures that your card will both remain "active" and also show perfect credit use.

Credit cards, with their high interest rates, are not substitutes for loans. Never use a credit card to borrow money, but instead pay the entire balance off within days of any purchase. In other words, don't use a credit card to buy anything that you couldn't buy with cash *on the same day*. If you are "low self-control super-shopper" who may be tempted to buy things you don't need (and can't afford), don't keep your credit card in your wallet – keep it at home, and only take it out for planned purchases.

Step 3 - The Down Payment

Once you have built up some savings or investments, and established a credit card or investment loan for longer than 6 months with perfect repayment history, you are ready to think about getting the loan you need (mortgages may require more time).

To improve your odds of acceptance, you must show your commitment to the loan by saving money to maximize your loan-to-value ratio, or LTV. The LTV ratio is the amount of money you put as a down payment on your purchase, compared to the amount of money you are borrowing. For example, if you are buying a $20,000 car and you are borrowing $20,000, the loan-to-value ratio is 100%. If you are buying the same car and putting $5000 toward a down payment, the loan-to-value ratio is 75% (5000/20,000). From the bank's perspective, the more money you put into the purchase, the more likely you are to pay, because the more of your own money (not the bank's money) you have to lose. For instance, if you borrow the full amount and don't pay, the worst you could lose is the vehicle; however, if you put $5000 of your own money down and don't pay, the worst you could lose is your $5000 *and* the vehicle!

From the lender's viewpoint, saving money for a down payment shows both good money management, and your serious intention to repay the loan.

In conclusion, proving your "financial maturity," means planning for future uncertainty by establishing a savings account or cashable investment. You also need to develop your credit worthiness by having a small investment loan or credit card, and have this credit "operating satisfactorily" by making consistent, on-time payments. Finally, save a reasonable down payment for the loan you want (ask you banker what is the minimum required).

Keep in mind that re-establishing great credit does not happen overnight. In general, a minimum of 6 months must pass before you even attempt to apply for a major loan or mortgage, with most lenders requiring at least 1 year. If you apply before this time, you will either be declined, or be approved with an astronomically high rate. Think of good credit as a work in progress. The longer that your good credit record is established, the better your chances for approval and preferred rates.

MONEY MANAGER CHECKLIST - SUMMARY

O 2 month's worth of living expenses in tangible liquid assets (cash in savings, cashable GICs, stocks, bonds, mutual funds etc.) in case of emergency.

O Have a credit product (credit card, loan etc.) and have had it "operating satisfactorily" with consistent, on-time payments for a minimum of 6 months – over 1 year preferred.

O Have low or $0 balance on all your existing credit products.

O Have saved a minimum 5% down payment toward your purchase (more may be required, depending upon your purchase).

If you have successfully completed the Money Manager Checklist above, you are ready to go to Chapter 2 – "Where to Apply, and When."

APPENDIX E

LIABILITIES WORKSHEET: SAMPLE

Name: John Doe	Credit Product	Company or Bank	Credit Limit	Balance	Monthly Required Payment
MTG (including Property Taxes) or RENT		HSBC		$119,000	$890
Credit Cards	Visa	Citibank	$5000	$3207	$96
	MC	WFF	$7500	$1200	$24
Dept. Store and Other Cards		Sears	$3000	$0	$0
Lines of Credit	Personal	HSBC	$12,000	$2340	$50
	Over draft	HSBC	$1000	$0	$0
Personal Loans	Car	HSBC		$9801	$252
	Boat	Citibank		$12,000	$229
Co-signed Loans					
Other	Income Taxes	Gov't		$2100	
TOTALS				$149,648	$1541

LIABILITIES WORKSHEET
(Photocopy & enlarge to use)

Name:

	Credit Product	Company or Bank	Credit Limit	Balance	Monthly Required Payment
MTG (including Property Taxes) or RENT					
Credit Cards					
Dept. Store and Other Cards					
Lines of Credit					
Personal Loans					
Co-signed Loans					
Other					
TOTALS					

Be kind to your banker : how to get the

3120001683034 BH

CPSIA information can be obtained at www.ICGtesting.com
Printed in the USA
LVOW111652290312

275322LV00011B/110/P